purl

poems by

Michele Evans

Finishing Line Press
Georgetown, Kentucky

purl

Copyright © 2025 by Michele Evans
ISBN 979-8-88838-843-3 First Edition
LCCN: 2025901581
All rights reserved under International and Pan-American Copyright Conventions. No part of this book may be reproduced in any manner whatsoever without written permission from the publisher, except in the case of brief quotations embodied in critical articles and reviews.

Publisher: Leah Huete de Maines
Editor: Christen Kincaid
Cover and Interior Art: Harrison Evans
Author Photo: Kennedy and Kendall Evans
Cover Design: Elizabeth Maines McCleavy

Order online: www.finishinglinepress.com
also available on amazon.com, barnesandnoble.com, bookshop.org, and other booksellers

Author inquiries and mail orders:
Finishing Line Press
PO Box 1626
Georgetown, Kentucky 40324
USA

Contents

i. swirl

aquaria 1

aria no. 1 2

aria no. 2 3

labyrinthia | in three parts 4

aeolia 8

athenia 9

laestrygonia 10

calliopeia 11

sestinia 12

aria no. 3 14

aria no. 4 15

malea 16

charybdia 17

aeaea 18

aria no. 5 20

aria no. 6 21

penelopia 22

anticlea 23

helenia 24

cytheria 25

sirenia | in two parts 26

ii. stitch

- melancholia 31
- nausicaa 32
- olivia 34
- musea: if homer's odyssey were her museum 35
- aria no. 7 36
- aria no. 8 37
- eurycleia 38
- domestica 40
- ogygia 41
- arachnia | in two parts 42
- aria no. 9 44
- aria no. 10 45
- diademia | in fifteen parts 46
- xenia 61

Notes 63
Acknowledgments 64
About the Artist 66
About the Author 67

for those thick spines
long lost in translation,
past voices flooding present,
bottled up sea glass blues,
cloudy futures still battling
demons, monsters, and selves...

"Soft purl the streams, the birds renew their notes,
And through the air their mingled music floats."

—Phillis Wheatley Peters, "An Hymn to the Evening"

i.

swirl

purl /pearl/

v. to eddy or curl as a shallow stream flows over stones.
n. a murmuring sound made by the motion of water.

aquaria

>/uh-kweh-ree-uh/ *n.* a tank, bowl, or other water-filled enclosure in which living fish or other aquatic animals and plants are kept (for public exhibition).

if you look carefully
    you just might see me
bearing water stories,
    horrors mixing
with my own transparency.

if you listen carefully
    you just might hear me
singing sea soliloquies,
    sorrows retracing
with my own legacy.

if you feel carefully
    you just might catch me
bottling up disparity,
    mirrors swirling
with my own therapy.

aria no. 1

/ah-ree-uh/ *n.* in music, a self-contained piece for one voice, normally part of a larger work.

floating and hidden—
in latin, the word insula
means isolated

aria no. 2

harnessed and muzzled,
riding the merry-go-round
of life's ups and downs

labyrinthia

/lab-rin-thee-ah/ *n.* a derivative of labyrinth, a complex system of paths or tunnels; a maze or a complicated situation.

when i was a child,
mama told me:

*sticks and stones
may break my bones
but words
will never hurt me.*

so i chose
a big grey stone
from a little tin bucket
not to throw
or break someone's bones
but to write on it—
like it was paper
one word
in permanent
black marker:

perspective.

and then
i chose
a simple, white card
pinned to
a rustic frame
propped up
on an easel made of sticks.

and
i walked
under a canopy
of crepe myrtle trees
—bright clusters
of fragrant fuchsia blossoms
and shiny dark leaves.

and
i walked
in circles
made of sticks and stones
going nowhere
and everywhere
at the same time
clutching
my big grey stone
and simple white card
that read:

keep your head
up
and your heart
open.

it was those words
not sticks and stones
that hurt me.
this time
mama was wrong.

when i was a child, mama told me: sticks and stones may break my bones but words will never hurt me. when i chose a big grey stone from a little tin bucket not to throw or break someone's bones but to write on it - like it was paper one word in permanent black marker: so i chose a big grey stone and then i chose a simple, white card pinned under a canopy of crepe myrtle trees - bright clusters of fragrant fuchsia blossoms and dark shiny leaves. and i walked under a canopy of crepe myrtle trees - and i walked in circles made of sticks and stones going nowhere and everywhere at the same time clutching my big grey stone and simple white card that read: keep your head up and your heart open. it was those words not sticks and stones that hurt me. mama was wrong this time. perspective perspective perspective perspective mama told me to keep your head up and your heart open, draw a simple, white time card pinned to a rustic crepe myrtle tree propped on an easel made of sticks. and the card read: sticks and stones may break my bones but words will never hurt me... when i was little it was like it was paper — this kind of thing was wrong so i chose a big stone from a little tin bucket not to throw or break someone's bones but to write one word in permanent black marker: perspective perspective perspective perspective. and i walked through lands, walked under a canopy of crepe myrtle trees and bright clusters of fragrant fuchsia blossoms and shiny sticks and stones going nowhere and everywhere at the same time carrying my big grey stone and simple white card that read: sticks and stones may break my bones but words will never hurt me.

aeolia

>/ay-oh-lee-ah/ *n.* in Greek mythology, the floating island where Aeolus, guardian of the winds, resides.

when clouds usher in
soft morning light,
she disappears

floating above air,
her hooves
searching for solid ground,

round and round trotting
everywhere and nowhere
all at once

unbridled—yet she dances
effortlessly under twinkling lights
to the carousel's lilt,

saddling the weight
of humans, large and small
on her back

but

when a familiar breeze blows,
and the night replaces day,
and the humans leave,
and the twinkling stops,
and the music silences,
and the roundabout slows,
she will reappear
from years of keeping
burdens hidden
deflection at its finest.

athenia

>/ah-then-ee-ah/ *n.* derivative of Athena, ancient Greek goddess associated with wisdom, handicraft, and warfare, and mentor to Odysseus.

who really needs saving? him or me? i know it's bad to wish lightning would strike him down, but i am tired of extending an olive branch, especially when it's so not deserved. i mean, is he even capable of loving me like the divine goddess i am? always the one to clean up the fallout from his foolery. i can see right through him and know he is not all that high and mighty. sometimes i just want to stab him with my gel manicured talons; but, in the end i always cave—throwing wisdom out to sea; so, i ask again: who really needs saving? him or me?

laestrygonia

/ly-stra-go-nee-ah/ *n.* the seaport village where the Laestrygones, a tribe of man-eating giants from ancient Greek mythology, lived.

i couldn't throw daggers
with my eyes anymore,
so i chiseled bits
of mother earth,
chunks of grey rock,
to hurl at him

and when the dust
from launched cannons
injected grey smoke
into my lungs cove,
i coughed up
every contact trace
memory of him

but when the rubble
refused to leave,
my grey heart dimmed—
i, buried underneath
a quarry of pain,
never learned to live
without him.

calliopeia

/kuh-ly-uh-pee-ah/ *n.* a derivative of Calliope, in Greek mythology, the muse of epic poetry.

i wail and warn,
sing and scream,
blare and blast,
pulse and pierce,
trumpet and toll,
four hundred years
without an orchestra
to amplify my arias
adrift in concert,
a cry caught
in a current
off course,
lost at sea
with no beacon
to deliver me
from intolerance
and isolation,
the only living
survivor willing
invisible heirs
nothing
but a ring
of dry brittle bones.

sestinia

/ses-ten-nee-ah/ *n.* a derivative of sestina, a patterned poem with six six-line stanzas and six end words.

her thoughts swirl like tiny shards of sand blown
across nearby dunes. as rays of soft morning light appear
through patches of clouds, her cracked hooves move away
from shadows, weighed down by tar. she is spooked when
guests scamper everywhere searching for solid ground, lost
on an island floating above a sea of invisible burdens.

through life's storms and seasons, she keeps these burdens
hidden, trapped in a pair of heavy woolen sacks. blown
dreams of her life, ripe with disappointment. years of lost
rights, lost loves, lost children, lost chances do not appear
to cripple her, for she is an expert in deflection, when
ever her heavy gait needs to become graceful in a way.

isolated—her black sand fills shores, an ideal getaway,
a tranquil isle perfect for shedding skins and burdens.
with each unforgiving ripple, the sea opens wide when
untamed winds threaten to steer curious strangers blown
off course towards her retreat before she can disappear
from bards who expose painful secrets of a paradise lost.

under a twinkling sky many moons later, no longer lost,
she will emerge a black beauty, unbridled, dancing in-a-way
to a carousel's lilt. learning to carry those who appear
harmless, round and round saddling their burdens
effortlessly until pieces of her majestic frame are blown
shattered and scattered by moans from an invisible wind.

when lost, blown away, burdens appear.

how long will it take for a different story to appear?
because herstory has a way of repeating itself. when
ever there is progress, another bag opens, more burdens
release, eroding shells of her past and present, lost
muzzled cries, like footprints tides have washed away,
leaving her thoughts to swirl like tiny shards of sand blown.

aria no. 3

silent cries for help
tied up in a woolen sack
swallowed by the sea

aria no. 4

frolicking flowers
in my garden—amnesia
replanting my pain

malea

/ma-lee-ah/ *n.* a Greek peninsula and a flowering plant.

i was hopeless, running away from home and him and hurt
when a lush overgrown island of lotus blossoms welcomed me

to a new dawn, after the ninth day the gods finally showed favor,
and i washed ashore, rescued by natives who would rehab me

far beyond the waves, my addiction took residence
with other diseased, until doctors prescribed me

daily sunray shots eventually fading the rope
bracelets i wore where he once tattooed me

with swallowed pills and rainwater i washed down
murky memories from pasts that punched me

hardest during night's silences when all patients
became prisoners to tremors, those that reminded me

of being enclosed, tied up, homebound in a darkened pod,
exposed only to brief flickers of sky when he fed me

platefuls of side-effects: windowless yellowed eyes,
slowed heartbeats, numb limbs supporting a weakened me,

on my knees, hands clasped shedding grief's residue,
an all you can eat buffet of worry, behind me

so, i rebelled and rebloomed, rose to the surface,
floating, feeling both resurrected and rapturous,

my petals showy, reviving and thriving
in rich loam, i, thick stemmed, honey skinned,

at last hopeful learned how to forgive…me.

charybdia

        /kuh-rib-dee-ah/ *n.* a derivative name for a whirlpool sea monster in Homer's *Odyssey*.

one.

this midnight beast compels my nervous stomach to howl as rosy fingertips
dive deeply into pools near the back of my throat. three times each day
i spew up sickness, whatever mom force-fed me before, this unhealthy
(life threatening ritual) way of carving too thick thighs, tree trunks
rooted in disguise because endless hundreds on worn tracks did nothing
for my never petite, never rock hard, never bikini ready bod,
so i flushed chunks, flesh outracing globs of bile, round and round until
eye won, till i was no longer (in)visible anymore.

two.

mom always said nothing good happens after midnight,
so when i get caught between rock and hard place i know she is right
before i tripped, facepalming with white porcelain from years ago,
too loudspeakers drowned out his true intentions as my innocence
grasped the frosted rosé he generously sent my way. a vile poisonous pinch
swirling round and round until melting on the glass floor, my shapeless body
by the narrow alleyway door, where laid out on my back i stared past nobody,
a faceless lout from a distorted reality, the roof above
disappearing into a blackened sky as he swallowed me whole.

three.

when mom released the refrain clogged in her windpipe, i discovered
the big rocks of her life metastasized. yellowed, like pages from a worn story,
she "survived" on a liquid diet cocktail, one part chemo, two parts faith,
with a splash of radiation, reducing her from trunk to twig, upchucking everything,
sometimes nothing, a nervous stomach feeding on what i use to starve.
swallowed whole by a [sic] headed monster, her wrinkly pink fingertips
pressed together in prayer refused to pay homage anymore so i watched her
life whirlpool down the drain littering the sea for one last midnight.

aeaea

/ay-ee-ah/ *n.* a mythological island said to be the home of the goddess-sorceress Circe.

i had no mama to show me round the kitchen
for she took her last breath as i took my first.

my skin honeyed and caramelized kept me in the big house,
away from my own, hidden from kin but not the ruthless one
always hovering above, a sunny master burning picked bolls.

mama didn't leave me no book of recipes, no kitchen gadget
manual, nothing to help this latchkey girl survive a life
of lonely, no stick figure dirt diagrams showing what to do
when wild, hungry eyes lick their chops, ready to feast on me.

sometimes, i, young and alone, could feel her magic in my marrow
bones, invisible hands guiding me as i drowned bitter collards in a pail
of ice water, before rolling their veined leaves into tight choke hold
bundles, cut and shredded like old greying moss hanging from a tree.

sometimes when i wielded her wooden staff in brews simmering
out of that old black cast iron cauldron set atop flames cackling,
her reflection appeared, patiently waiting to help me cradle
enough ham hock bones and field pickins to feed an entire army,
ravenous weary soldiers home from yet another battle.

sometimes the bubbling greens and animal limbs sent smoke signals,
an sos of sorts, leading platoons of predators, along a scented trail,
of breadcrumbs, charmed musical notes, through a dense wood
to my enchanted fortress, a sumptuous banquet table feast
set before them, where without hesitation, they devoured like pigs,
gorging and grunting "holy moly, this sure is some good chow."

sometimes after plates licked clean, the sound from tamed bellies
injected with itis, a circadian snoring from the snouts of soldiers
lulled to a deep sleep in a sty of temporary shallow graves, granted me
security, permission to shut my eyes if only for a few brief moments.

this daily regimen worked well until it didn't, until the day
i felt his hands, not my mother's, wrapped around my slender waist
first and then over my mouth muzzling screams that followed.
there was no survival manual that day, no recipe, no spell, no trance to stop
that pig from feasting on the aroma coming from my copper pot.

nothing to stop him from injecting me with a different itis.
nothing to break the curse for mamas who birth half-sisters.

aria no. 5

ring of broken bones
ring in my ears—drums unplugged
ring around my neck

aria no. 6

her chilly nature
boiled and reduced to slush
verses on a page

penelopia

> /pe-nell-oh-pee-ah/ n. a derivative name for Penelope, the wife of Odysseus and mother of Telemachus.

oh, how i wish my son was a mama's boy
so he could learn to love and not destroy
a women's heart like his father did mine
twenty years ago when he left to fight
a battle far from our home's coastline
leaving me alone to raise his son right.

after waving bye, i still saw his face
each time i swaddled our tiny infant son
too young to remember his father's embrace
to know our family was over before it begun.

working several jobs kept us off welfare
too busy to follow his posts, tweets, snaps
of infidelity floating in the nightly air
rumors about her making me collapse

on hands, praying for him to come back
to our rough hood, a concrete island rife
with strife and drunken suitors in a pack
lurking, slinging each corner about that life

ready to make my boy their new trainee
in their felonious class on manhood
before he drops out to take a journey
chasing after the king who never could

searching for a father who didn't drown,
the one to show him how to respect
so he will not abuse his name and crown
so he will not treat women with neglect.

oh, how i wish my love was a mama's boy
who would come home and bring me joy.

anticlea

/ante-clee-ah/ *n.* queen of Ithaca and mother of Odysseus.

i told him too much of anything is almost always a bad thing,
just because there are too many fish in the sea doesn't mean
you should catch one for every day of the week, except sunday,
because one day, six heads will scoop you up and eat you alive.

this is not the moment i have been waiting for—hades
is a mother's hospital waiting room, a dreadful place
where restless soles pace, where twenty minutes feels
like twenty years waiting for my sons' return from
bird watching, jogging, wandering, while i sit waiting.

why don't you pick on someone your own size, i moaned, trapped
inside one cave's soundproof walls. bet this lawless monster swears
nobody did this. contradicting eye phone witness and millions
who heard my baby boy cry, choking out, "mama, i can't breathe."

helenia

>/hel-len-ee-ah/ *n.* a derivative of the name Helen, Queen of Sparta, described in Greek mythology as the most beautiful woman in the world.

her face black and bruised did not launch one thousand ships
or even ignite a ten-year war between nations, trojan and greek
soldiers, hiding out in wooden horses playing clever tricks,
tearing down walled cities, turning the once mighty into the weak.

her face black and bruised, a precious skull crushed by her master,
branded scars on display, plastered on wanted posters—beware!
an offer, a cash reward for her immediate return to her captor
because talking heads and mirrors believed her dangerous not fair.

her face black and bruised eventually ignited a civil war
when her nightly campaign to free hundreds of the enslaved
from the south, hiding them underground behind a safe door
escaping a dog whistle, chain lashing, and hanging grave.

her face once plastered on posters will soon grace dollar bills
for her efforts to break down slavery's walls with epic trips
guided by a star and faith from the eastern shore through hills
upstate, freeing many once shackled to one thousand ships.

cytheria

/sith-air-ree-ah/ *n.* a derivative of an Ionian island near Cape Malea in Homer's *Odyssey*.

are there
no safe spaces
for girls? no places where
predators can't prey, no?
no schools or pools, pages,
stages, where girls
may play?

free from
evil and fear?
no safe spaces for girls,
places where faces six centuries
later stop launching ships
like toys to be
played with?

sirenia | in two parts

/cy-re-nee-ah/ n. a derivative of the Sirens from Greek mythology, half-bird and half woman "dangerous" maidens whose singing lured sailors to shipwreck near their rocky isle.

sooner or later
most of us will be forced to live a double life,
hide what was once meaningful
and reveal what has now become meaningless,
but which half note should i sing about?
which half will liberate and make me whole?

        plummeting

                silence

        from the sky

                and then

        my pilot half

                shrieks

        feathers

                suffocating

        through clouds

                obstructed

        before

                gills

        crashing

                my seafarer half

        into rocks

                pulled

        below

                forever.

                                                            sooner or
                                                         later most
                                                      of us will be
   forced   to live a double life
   hide what was   once meaningful reveal
       what is now   meaningless but which
                half note   should i sing about?
                  which half   note will make me
                    whole?   plummeting silence
                    from the sky and then my pilot half
                 shrieks, feathers suffocating through
              clouds obstructed before gills crashing my
                 seafarer half into rocks pulled below forever.

                                                       sooner or
                   later most of us will be   forced to live a double
                      life, hide what was once   meaningful, reveal
                           what is now meaningless. but which half note
                              should i sing about? which half note will
                                 make me whole? plummeting
                                    from the sky, my
                                       pilot half
                                       feathers
                                       through
                                        clouds
                                        before
                                        crashing
                                        into rocks
                                        below.
                                        silence and
                                        then shrieks
                                        suffocating
                                        obstructing gills
                                        my seafarer
                                        half pulled
                                        forever.

ii.

stitch

purl /pearl/

v. to weave or knit with a reverse stitch looping along a border or edge.
n. thread made of gold or silver wire.

melancholia

>/meh-len-coal-ee-ah/ *n.* a severe form of depression, characterized by bodily complaints, feelings of hopelessness, and loss of energy.

i rewrite their stories to avoid sharing my own
autobiography—truths hiding in plain sight
behind archetypes greek, classical in nature
so different from my heritage and culture
and yet also very much the same.

i recast their sorrows in stanzas, statues, and stones,
replacing my reality with illusions—allusions pouring
out from a grecian urn, a cocktail mixture
one part past, two parts present.

i reweave their threads old and new,
black and white, cliched and coded messages
lost for years at sea, trapped glass bottles
floating freely but never reaching final destinations.

i rewear their sandals and shackles donned
by female forces from the past and present
to navigate my future, never forgetting
always remembering what they look like.

nausicaa

/nous-see-kah/ *n.* in the Odyssey, a princess who aids Odysseus near the coast of a Greek isle.

i am waiving my flag
even if it's not white anymore.

before he washed up on my shores,
laundry was a chore i didn't mind,
but now, no matter what i do—
i can't remove his stain. bruises
and blemishes over time fade
but never really go away.

i tried every store-bought detergent:
no oxyclean or tide could clorox
the memory of that day i met him
clinging for life at water's edge.

i thought he needed saving, i was wrong.
and now i must air out my dirty laundry
in public, for this pain is more than i
(or anyone) should ever wear in private.

i beat my flag, a pearly white linen shift,
to death against the isle's jagged shore
line, an attempt to remove the residue
from splatters—his sticky sweat and seed.

i pound my knuckles bleeding oozing
drops, like crushed grapes. thin cottony
threads splitting seams wide open against
the stony grey washboard of rocks.

i hang my soaked fabric from a tree to dry,
the relentless sunlight exposing its secrets,
still soiled and stiff, waltzing to the
wind's anthem, ghost of a moment past.

blemishes and bruises over time
fade but never really go away,
the toughest stains remain invisible,
you can't erase what you can't see.

so, i am waving my flag
even if it's not white anymore.

olivia

/oh-liv-ee-uh/ n. a feminine name derived from the Latin word oliva meaning olive or olive tree.

she was crushed bitter, briny
until she found wisdom lurking
in the place where the pit resides.

oh, live she heard the swirling
spirit whisper, removing heart's
ache reviving her rancid insides.

musea: if homer's *odyssey* were her museum

/myooz-ee-ah/ *n.* a derivative of a building housing artifacts.

exhibit no. 4:
at the fore, a statuesque four wheeled quarter bred for rescuing
a stony-faced forsaken queen hidden behind *hell in* a wall of cement.

exhibit no. 3:
a triumvirate's libretto, a blackened note, trill and a *sigh winds* perched atop
stony parchment, cemented arias silenced by their prey.

exhibit no. 2:
twin pedestals, stone faced, yellow eyed statuesque mountains cemented
and tame, a portico protection from *sirs. see* the threat of wild animals.

exhibit no 1:
a single stone post, rough-hewn, ripened smooth, an oiled trunk *penny*
colored with twenty-year old, cemented roots, a gnarly pillow of nightmares.

the final exhibit:
a songbook, refrains inspired by forgotten pasts and futures, a paper *muse*(um)
of sorts, restoring cemented hearts from the rotten timbers of life.

aria no. 7

cocktail recipe:
shattered limbs—muddled man flesh,
water, and brandy

aria no. 8

her grief unmanaged
a portal to hades realm
cursed forever more

eurycleia

/yur-ree-clee-ah/ *n.* a loyal maid who nursed and raised Odysseus.

it's not like he abandoned me; and now i don't care
about him, or you, or the other dozen or so maids,
but when his heart sailed away leaving this island,
betraying his throne, i was hurt and lost,
unstable, unrecognizable, unloved, unable to see,
unraveled, and over time i became hardened and cruel.

it's not like you don't know the rules
the best defense: pretend like you don't care,
be still, like an anchored war vessel at sea,
be silent, like secrets trapped under made
bedsheets in haste. haven't i suffered enough loss?
who knows if he'll ever return? and where will i land?

it's not like living on this remote island,
pledging blind loyalty to an absent king—a cruel
husband, plagued, possessed, fighting a losing
battle with ptsd, has left me without a care.
some of my life's happiest moments he made
what can i possibly do or say to make you see?

it's not like you are the one drowning at sea
all the time. life on this blissful island
is not always bad. i, my worst enemy, made
this bed and you can't ask me to change the rules
because after all these years, i still care
about him and believe our king is not lost.

it's not like it's time to surrender, all's not lost,
i know there must be a way to make him see
he is his own worst enemy, a way to make him care
about his kingdom and family, his island's
riches and beauty, once again. cure his cruel
heart and restore him to how he was first made.

it's all been a waste of time, everything you ever made
us believe. i use to blame him but you are the one lost.
how will i ever trust again now that you have become cruel
after decades of loving what we both hate? can't you see
how his absence swallowed us whole on this island
splitting our souls into pieces without a single care?

domestica

/doh-mes-tikah/ *n.* an epithet for those who live a life of toil.

weaving their threads
white lies shrouding our own
black truths into silence

brewing bitter stems
roots plucked from earth's womb
destroying seeds never planted

mopping up hollow grounds
where our fallen souls once
lie bloody, beaten, and broken

hanging from gnarly oaks
twelve dresses all in a row
each still twitching feet

ogygia

/oh-gig-ea-ah/ *n.* an island mentioned in Homer's *Odyssey*, home of the nymph Calypso.

god sent a rainbow,
a clear message wrapped in glass:
be still and let him go.
immediately, i wanted to write back:
please, no!
because i had saved him—
not his patient wife,
not his desirable mistress,
not even his baby mama,
i, an all of the above wannabe, had saved him—
so i wrote a different note,
pushed it out into a dead sea
like the raft he used to escape me,
and i tried instead to just   be
still.
inside the glass, the scroll reply:
dear immortality: just. let. me. die.
when nobody wrote back,
i collapsed where sand and sea lie,
waiting to exhale violet blue notes
from melancholy's elegy,
waiting to unravel threads of juniper
from despair's shroud,
waiting to stoke peppery flakes
from grief's pyre...
until one day, a circle of friends—
guilt, shame, and pride
emerged from the cave inside
to circle and pray over my lifeless body
like phases of the moon struck
speak—easy angelic melodies
finally lifting the weight of the world
from my shoulders.
so full of grace
bottled in afterglow,
i finally floating let him   go.

arachnia | in two parts

/ah-rack-nee-ah/ *n.* a derivative for a human weaver turned into a spider; a black out poem from Emily Wilson's translation of Homer's *Odyssey*

pity. no one spoke
unkindly, blame
cheated hope
but her mind,
a mighty loom
said, *be patient;*
this winding-sheet
shrouded us
at night
by torchlight.
for three long seasons
there,
unraveling
his heart.

arachnia

      /ah-rack-nee-ah/ n. a derivative for a human weaver turned
      into a spider; a black out poem from Emily Wilson's translation of
      Homer's *Odyssey*

pity. no one spoke;
      unkindly.

                      blame

    cheated
  hope
      her mind

a mighty loom
                said   ,

                be patient;
                this winding-sheet.

            shroud   e
            d

  at night by torchlight
for three long years

      there, unraveling

      his heart   .

aria no. 9

places her mind
travels to when he is lost
in her loving arms

aria no. 10

beginnings are not
simply endings in disguise;
they are eyes unveiled

diademia | in fifteen parts

/dye-ah-dem-ee-ah/ *n.* a diadem, a royal headband or crown;
in poetry, 15 linked sonnets, a sonnet redoublé or sonnet corona.

i.

because he said she could not wear a crown
her mama wove one a top her head.
squirming on the bed's edge when mama said,
be quiet my child, chin up, don't look down
each time mama stabbed her scalp parting brown
foray (4a) with a steely tipped comb, she shed
tears until that first plait emerged to spread
a toothy smile across her once tattooed frown;

for decades her story like others loc'd
under layers matted with lye and blue
magic, lie hidden—still—buried gemstones
talk, like waves crashing her verses ad hoc
reclaiming ancient tales of a tamed "shrew,"
to honor her, forgotten at the thrones.

ii.

to honor her forgotten at the thrones
for she was one of the firsts to fill us
with letters and poems on "various
subjects, religious and moral" in tones;
sold into slavery, stripped from her home
this west african woman named phillis
wheatley, the first literary genius
wore a cloth bonnet crowning her dome,

taught young to read and write well above norms
emulating latin poets of old
this gem bought a key to unlock her cage:
she hid her story in classical forms
freeing her hands to guide the pen strokes, bold
swirls moving forcefully across the page.

iii.

swirls moving forcefully across the page,
across continents, time zones, centuries
to a contest held amongst deities
who used her face like a mirror to gage
women's beauty, regardless of one's age
for the goddess who won the golden prize
creating a hell in today's world's eyes
of hostile men looking for wars to wage,

like the ten-year battle between the greeks
and the trojans over helen the queen
of sparta whose face launched one thousand ships
tossed back and forth through crashing waves, her shrieks
unheard, misinterpreted, lost between
worlds where beauty wars still apocalypse.

iv.

worlds where beauty wars still apocalypse,
this nymph lived an island life of lonely
where the cowrie shells kept her company
until the day she saw his broken ship
and rescued him from the sea's deadly grip.
for many years she cared for nobody
in her smooth scalloped caves while waves crashed by
marking each day after the moon's eclipse;

she spent her day collecting pearls to weave
with palm fronds and seaweed into a pair
of crowns, wedding rings, binding them as one
until he tired and wanted to leave
her for his true wife and his only heir,
her golden wreaths burning under the sun.

v.

her golden wreaths burning under the sun
light bounces off locks hissing and coiling,
protecting her, the aegis armoring
her bronzy skin in battles lost and won
because she counseled gods, kings, men who shun
wisdom in war where common sense missing
in action, flags atop capitols flying,
crowning this greek goddess, the grey eyed one,

a woman, mentoring men on matters
of fact, who would have thought that possible?
a divine counselor could be female
with an owl not a chip on her shoulders
wielding a spear, covered in virgin wool
then and now she is who we should regale.

vi.

then and now she is who we should regale
for her gifts fill air with sweet melodies
ovid and homer used her expertise
this mother of sirens, beyond the pale
songbirds, and chief of all muses who hails
from the mount, queen of epic poetry
striking her writing pen in higher keys
birthing classical forms in epic tales

where bards, poets say her name to invoke
and infuse their tablets with her voice
amused, this eloquent one of twelve said,
by honoring my crowning gifts bespoke
lyrical verses of multiple choice,
a wellspring from this epic fountainhead.

vii.

a wellspring from this epic fountainhead
tempting sailors with enchanting music,
charming zephyr winds, destructive shipwrecks
to litter their rocky island with dead
bodies of men, boys, married or unwed
shards of shell and bone sharpened to bedeck
a floating trap house for the "lunatic"
trio, a grecian nuclear warhead

ready to attack whenever threatened
perhaps these creatures are not dangerous
but a detour desirable off course,
their crowning achievement forced to defend
themselves from men and vile acts treasonous
in life where nature ends by trojan horse.

viii.

in life where nature ends by trojan horse
this monster of the sea did not have sic
heads, did not port sailors to river styx
did not force those to travel a death course,
did not span twelve feet in air, this force,
once a nymph in love now by a charmed trick
forever crowned by a lonely homesick
goddess lacking empathy and remorse,

said, *if i can't have that man then no one can.*
so now this sick headed shetaur with fangs
cutting tools of the sea, six at a time
from fishermen boats, a king's caravan,
a greek blessing in disguise for the gangs
lying in wait by the whirlpool's prime.

ix.

lying in wait by the whirlpool's prime
eruption to pull a ship down below
to the depths of the seafloor even though
helping her father was her only crime,
and punishment came swiftly on a dime
to the poor young maiden of the sea, woe
begone her hourglass figure and glow
reduced into a salty glob of slime,

a never-ending cycle of past pains
to probate a generational curse
robbing girls, women of their right to wealth
unfairly taxed on net capital gains
that empty the dowry, chest, and purse
compromising their well-being and health.

x.

compromising their well-being and health
this twelve put the needs of their king ahead
of their own, to cook his chow, make his bed,
nurse babes, mop floors, weaving his shroud in stealth
a bad hand of cards in life to be dealt
no hearts or diamonds, clubs and spades instead
to beat the rugs, grind the stone, bake the bread
a life dedicated to those who felt

no obligation to appreciate
or soothe their calloused hands, broken backs, sore
feet, bruised souls for cleaning up the blood mess
when suitors slaughtered in mass by their great
king, now there's no list of chores anymore
for the dozen hanging crowns in distress.

xi.

for the dozen hanging crowns in distress
your deaths will not be in vain, your stories
will be shared in future allegories
of song and printed letterpress.
your souls will be welcomed here bodiless
to a space where shadows search for glories
in air thickened with death, doom, and disease
undeserved pension for your faithfulness;

a broken heart—not neck, my ticket here
to mourn my son never coming back home,
every mother's broad burden to carry.
*what if i could go back in time and clear
their names?* the maidens would be free to roam
somewhere other than a cemetery.

xii.

somewhere other than a cemetery
is where she should long to be, but her mind
and body plagued too sick to quarantine
in solitary confinement ferry
her back to books of spells in her library
and the cypress table with herbs to grind
using her mortar and pestle spellbind
to cure her sadness with a potpourri

wreath made from grass and leaves the illusion
her seclusion fake, his divine love real
squeals of delight filled the empty air
when he said bye a foregone conclusion
returning to life on his emerald isle hill
and leaving her with nothing but an heir.

xiii.

and leaving her with nothing but an heir
her husband-king left them for two decades
to battle many from troy to hades
collecting booty and war souvenirs:
a lotus, a lout's eye, and love affairs
the topics of bards' instagram charades
traveling the sea like this jack of all trades
leaving her with island and son to care;

for all single queens know how hard this task
can be under the glare of prying eyes
from a son, suitors, twelve maids, and in-laws.
this shiny penny learned to wear a mask
learned to outwit, outplay, outlast her spies
not for the fame or fortune or applause.

xiv.

not for the fame or fortune or applause
did she swear an oath to tell the whole truth
about the day when that man stole her youth
when he washed up on her shore fleeing claws
from a trident, a sea monster's jaws.
this stranger, whose real name should be uncouth
not king, or father, or husband, or son
when he reached for her dress made of thin gauze;

he did not care she was only a child,
a daughter, sister, or future mother
his only care was to release his seed
and keep the secret of how he defiled
her crown before the sea tried to smother
him whole and all his unspeakable deeds.

xv.

him whole and all his unspeakable deeds
have made each of us stronger than before.
prose from our sisters' past shelf the bookstore,
poems from mothers' past string our prayer beads
with ribboned pom-poms, we learned to cheerlead
for girls to keep breaking the ceiling floor
here and there, high and low; forevermore,
women around the world will not concede

until this chain of events now broken
is repaired, so this world loves all girls
from cities, villages, and every town
in between, till she is not some token
commodity who wears a string of pearls
because he said she could not wear a crown.

xenia

/zen-nee-ah/ *n.* the ancient Greek concept of hospitality.

oh, the gifts we bear
curses wrapped up as blessings
wineskin presents
pages brimming with songs
muffled voices rarely heard.

Notes

"musea: if homer's *odyssey* were her museum" takes its inspiration from Rachel Mennies' "If the Barn Were Her Museum."

"arachnia" is a blackout poem using page 123 from Book 2: "A Dangerous Journey" from Emily Wilson's translation of Homer's *Odyssey*.

"diademia: ii" borrows language from the title of Phillis Wheatley Peters's first volume of poetry, *Poems on Various Subjects, Religious and Moral*.

"diademia: xiii" references the tagline "outwit, outplay, outlast" from the television series *Survivor*.

Acknowledgments

Thank you to the following anthologies, journals, and magazines for publishing earlier versions of these poems.

Artemis, Volume XXX: "melancholia"
The ASP Bulletin: "anticlea"
Maryland Literary Review: "aeaea"
The Mid-Atlantic Review: "sirenia"
Sky Island Journal: "musea"
Tangled Locks Journal: "charybdia"
The Write Launch: "labyrinthia," "laestrygonia," "ogygia"
Yellow Arrow Journal, Elevate, Volume IX, No. 1: "malea"

"anticlea" was nominated for a Pushcart Prize and Best of the Net Award and won first place in *The ASP Bulletin* Poetry Contest, judged by Saida Agostini and Teri Ellen Cross Davis.

Simply put, none of this would be possible without my faith and family.

When I was six years old, my family helped me publish my first book. My mom, LaVarne, typed the story I scribbled in my Hello Kitty journal. Keith, my older brother, drew stick figure illustrations. And my dad, Arthur, bound everything together with a stapler. Together, we produced three copies of *A Christmas Memory*: one for me to read to my stuffed animals and dolls, one for safe keeping in a box of mementos and souvenirs, and one for the library at my school Markham Elementary. I still remember the excitement I felt when the librarian embellished my book with a call number, checkout card, and library pocket before placing it in circulation.

Several decades later, a much larger family has helped me publish this book. In addition to my parents and brother, I am incredibly blessed to have love and support from my husband, Shawn, and our children Kennedy, Harrison, and Kendall. When I finally picked up the pen again after years of being a wife, mother, teacher, coach, scout leader, and event planner, they gifted me space so I could make up for lost time. In their own way, each helped me as I learned how to become a writer again. I will be forever grateful to them: *purl's* first beta readers, editors, publicists, and illustrator. A world of thanks to my son Harrison for creating my blue queen, the stunning portrait gracing the book's cover, and the line art on the inside pages.

Since the idea for this poetry collection came to life after years of teaching Homer's classic epic *The Odyssey*, I would be remiss if I didn't acknowledge my Broad Run High School family, particularly the community of writers and educators in the English department and the students in my English 9 and Creative Writing classes. A special shout-out goes to Beth Konkoski, a colleague and dear friend, for giving me thoughtful feedback, holding me accountable to self-imposed deadlines, and helping me navigate the world of publishing.

As a lifelong learner, I have so much gratitude for the Northern Virginia Writing Project's Summer Institute (an affiliate of the National Writing Project) at George Mason University, in Fairfax, Virginia, formerly led by Sarah E. Rickless; the Keats-Shelley Memorial House in Rome, Italy, for sponsoring two online poetry workshops led by Moira Egan; and The Writer's Center in Bethesda, Maryland, for offering a poetry chapbook course led by Meg Eden. Many of the poems in *purl* were first drafted in these spaces.

Thank you to my ever-expanding writing family for amplifying my voice. I am indebted to *Tangled Locks, The Write Launch, Artemis Journal, ASP Bulletin, Maryland Literary Review, Mid-Atlantic Review, Sky Island Journal,* and *Yellow Arrow* for giving ten of these poems their first homes. To Hannah Grieco, Elizabeth Hazen, and Rose Solari from Alan Squire Publishing for nominating "anticlea" for a 2023 Pushcart Prize and Best of the Net in 2024. To Teri Ellen Cross Davis and Saida Agostini for selecting "anticlea" as the 2023 winner of the *ASP Bulletin* Poetry Contest. To Brooke C. Obie, Julia Tagliere, and Nathan Leslie for featuring me at my first readings in the Washington D.C. metropolitan area. To The Inner Loop and The Watering Hole for welcoming me into your literary families. To the Peterson and Evans families, my lifelong friends/sisters from Hayfield and Smith, and every person who has encouraged me over the years.

Thank you to those who paved the way for me and others: Maya Angelou, Gwendolyn Brooks, Lucille Clifton, Rita Dove, Nikki Giovanni, Zora Neale Hurston, June Jordan, Audre Lorde, Toni Morrison, Sonia Sanchez, Ntozake Shange, Natasha Trethewey, Alice Walker, Dorothy West, and Phillis Wheatley Peters.

Finally, thank you to the entire team at Finishing Line Press for publishing *purl* and placing it in circulation for readers around the world.

About the Artist

Harrison Evans is a self-taught artist from Virginia. Working with a primarily monochromatic palette, he specializes in digital and body art. Fueled by creativity and passion, this emerging illustrator aspires to use his art to enrich, educate, and empower those in his community and beyond.

About the Author

Michele Evans, a fifth-generation Washingtonian (D.C.), is a writer, teacher, and adviser for *Unbound*, an award-winning Northern Virginia high school literary magazine. This Pushcart Prize and Best of the Net nominee studied at Smith College, King's College London, and the Graduate School at the University of Maryland. Her poems have appeared in *Artemis Journal, The ASP Bulletin, Maryland Literary Review, Mid-Atlantic Review, Spoken Black Girl Magazine, Yellow Arrow Journal, Zora's Den,* and elsewhere. This Watering Hole fellow and Teacher Consultant for the Northern Virginia Writing Project lives online at www.awordsmithie.com. *purl* is her first poetry collection.

www.ingramcontent.com/pod-product-compliance
Lightning Source LLC
Chambersburg PA
CBHW030057170426
43197CB00010B/1561